MARCO POLO
Overland to Medieval China

MARCO POLO
Overland to Medieval China

Clint Twist

RSVP
RAINTREE
STECK-VAUGHN
PUBLISHERS
The Steck-Vaughn Company

Austin, Texas

Published by Raintree Steck-Vaughn Publishers, an imprint of Steck-Vaughn Company

Editors: Su Swallow, Shirley Shalit
Designer: Neil Sayer
Production: Jenny Mulvanny
Consultant: Jon von der Heide, Drew University

Maps and illustrations: Brian Watson, Linden Artists

Library of Congress Cataloging-in-Publication Data
Twist, Clint.
        Marco Polo: overland to medieval China / Clint Twist.
            p.   cm. — (Beyond the horizons)
        Includes bibliographical references and index.
        ISBN 0-8114-7251-5
        1. Polo, Marco, 1254-1323? — Journeys — Juvenile literature. 2. Voyages and
travels — Juvenile literature. 3. Explorers — Italy — Biography — Juvenile literature.
4. China — Description and travel — Juvenile literature. [1. Polo, Marco, 1254-1323?
2. Explorers. 3. Voyages and travels.] I. Title. II. Series: Beyond the horizons.
G370.P9T88   1994
915.104'25—dc20   93-30744
                                                                                       CIP AC

Printed in Hong Kong
Bound in the United States
1 2 3 4 5 6 7 8 9 0 LB 99 98 97 96 95 94 93

Acknowledgments

For permission to reproduce copyright material the author and publishers gratefully acknowledge the following:

Cover (top left) The Ancient Art & Architecture Collection, (top middle) Michael Holford, (left middle) Werner Forman Archive, (bottom left) Robert Harding Picture Library, (below right) Bodleian Library, Oxford.
Title page Bibliothèque Nationale, Paris/Robert Harding Picture Library **page 4** (top) Werner Forman Archive, (bottom) Ronald Sheridan, Ancient Art & Architecture Collection **page 5** Michael Holford **page 6** (top) e.t. archive, (bottom) Robert Harding Picture Library/Bodleian Library, Oxford, MS Bodley 264 **page 8** Mary Evans Picture Library **page 9** (top) Ronald Sheridan, Ancient Art & Architecture Collection, (bottom) Paul Trummer, The Image Bank **page 10** (top) Sally Morgan, Ecoscene, (bottom) Werner Forman Archive **page 11** Ira Block, The Image Bank **page 12** Ronald Sheridan, Ancient Art & Architecture Collection **page 13** Ronald Sheridan, Ancient Art & Architecture Collection **page 14** Robert Harding Picture Library **page 15** Bibliothèque Nationale, Paris/Robert Harding Picture Library **page 16** (top) Guido Alberto Rossi, The Image Bank, (bottom) Pierrette Collomb, The Hutchison Library **page 17** Robert Harding Picture Library **page 18** Robert Harding Picture Library **page 20** (top) Dr Baer, Zefa, (bottom) Andrew Ward, Life File **page 21** Ross Greetham, Robert Harding Picture Library **page 22** Dave Brinicombe, The Hutchison Library **page 23** Robert Harding Picture Library **page 24** (top) The Hutchison Library, (bottom) Werner Forman Archive **page 25** (top) Al Giddings, The Image Bank, (middle) Robert Harding Picture Library, (bottom) Werner Forman Archive **page 26** (top) e.t. archive, (bottom) B Moser, The Hutchison Library **page 27** (top) Ronald Sheridan, Ancient Art & Architecture Collection, (bottom) Robert Harding Picture Library/Bodleian Library, Oxford, MS Bodley 264 **page 29** (top) Sally Morgan, Ecoscene, (middle) Michael Holford, (bottom left) Robert Harding Picture Library, (bottom right) Stephen Marks, The Image Bank **page 30** Sally Morgan, Ecoscene **page 31** (top) Woodhead, The Hutchison Library, (bottom) Orion Press/Zefa **page 32** Heather Angel, Biofotos **page 33** Ronald Sheridan, Ancient Art & Architecture Collection **page 34** (top) e.t. archive, (bottom) Tony Waltham, Robert Harding Picture Library **page 35** Werner Forman Archive **page 36** Robert Harding Picture Library **page 37** (top) Werner Forman Archive, (middle) Michael Holford, (bottom) Werner Forman Archive **page 38** (top) Gerald Cubitt, Bruce Coleman Ltd, (middle) Peter Jackson, Bruce Coleman Ltd, (bottom) Werner Forman Archive **page 39** (top) Robert Harding Picture Library, (bottom) Ronald Sheridan, Ancient Art & Architecture Collection **page 41** Robert Harding Picture Library/Bibliotheque Nationale, Paris **page 42** (top, bottom) Ronald Sheridan, Ancient Art & Architecture Collection **page 43** e.t. archive

Contents

Introduction

An oriental image of Marco Polo. His hat marks him as a European.

This book is about Marco Polo, an Italian who spent his boyhood in Venice. In 1271, while Marco was still a teenager, his father took him on an incredible journey far beyond the known world, to meet the lord of a mighty empire. More than 20 years later, Marco Polo finally returned home, and soon joined the Venetian Army. He was captured, and made a prisoner of war. While in prison, he met a Frenchman whom he entertained with stories of his travels to China and India. The Frenchman was a writer, and he wrote Marco's stories down. And this is how *The Travels of Marco Polo - A Description of the World* first came to be written. Marco's book was a best-seller. Printing was not yet known in Europe so copies were made by hand. The book was translated into different languages and many people read it with wonder. Asia was now no longer a complete mystery, a vague area somewhere off the edge of the map. It was a real place, full of strange sights and customs but recognizably a civilized society.

Behind the headlines

In one sense, *The Travels of Marco Polo* was just good journalism, researched and written by two men who were lucky enough to be in the right place at the right time. Marco's account

Horizons

After reading this book, you may want to find out more about some aspect of Marco's journey. Or you may become interested in a particular place or topic. At the end of some of the chapters you will find **Horizons** boxes. These boxes list some of the important people, places, ideas, and objects that are not described in this book, but which were nevertheless part of Marco Polo's world. By looking them up in the index of other reference books, you will be able to discover more about Marco and his time.

This is believed to have been Marco Polo's house in Venice.

contained plenty to excite his readers. He had journeyed to the ends of the earth, to the sources of the fabulous wealth of Asia. There is little surprise that he had plenty of good stories to tell, especially as his subject was a very topical one. During the early part of the 13th century, the sudden rise of the Mongol Empire had brought Asia closer to Europe than it had ever been before. Many, remembering battles against the Mongol warriors who invaded eastern Europe, would have said that Asia was too close for comfort. Now here was a book by someone who had actually been a guest of the Mongol emperor.

However, in another sense, Marco's book reveals the spirit of Europe at this time. After centuries of conflict and destruction, Europe had at last become reasonably peaceful and prosperous. Marco belonged to a new Europe, which was beginning to show a serious interest in the world beyond its borders.

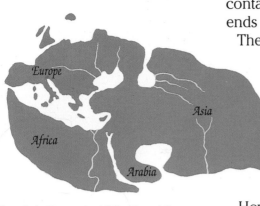

People in Europe had little idea of the world outside Europe until Marco Polo traveled to Asia.

Dreams of riches

There are several reasons for exploring foreign lands. Two important ones are conquest and trade. Marco had no dreams of conquest; he was concerned only with trade. But *The Travels* is much more than just a series of travelers' tales; it is a serious attempt to describe the non-European world to Europeans.

This is the real value of Marco's book. It was the first real proof that the fabulous riches of India and China actually existed. The goal of the great voyages of exploration two centuries later was to gain direct access to these riches. Christopher Columbus read *The Travels of Marco Polo*, and used it to plan the voyage that discovered America. At the time, only a few people believed Marco Polo's stories, but we now know that much of what he said was reasonably accurate. His book provides a fascinating insight into distant lands, in a time long since past.

The Grand Canal in Venice.

The Historical Background

Medieval Italian clerks at work.

A view of Marco Polo's departure from Venice painted 100 years after his death.

A teenage traveler

Marco Polo was born in Venice, Italy, in 1254. His father, Niccolo, was a prosperous merchant who imported luxury goods from Asia. When Marco was six years old, his father sailed off one day to Constantinople (now called Istanbul), and did not come back for nine years. Young Marco was left at home with his mother.

As the son of a wealthy merchant, Marco would have received some education. He was probably taught to read and write, but there were no storybooks for him to read. Printing was still unknown in Europe, and books had to be copied out by hand. Marco's main reading material was probably cargo lists and letters from his father. More importantly, for a trader's son, Marco would also have been taught his numbers, how to work out prices and convert foreign currency into Venetian money.

Some time before Marco's 16th birthday, his mother was taken ill and died. Shortly afterward, Marco's father returned home. He stayed in Venice for two years before setting out on another voyage. This time he took his son with him rather than leave him at home alone. Marco Polo was just 17 years old when he left Venice for the first time in his life. He would be nearly 42 years old when he saw Venice again.

Venice – a commercial superpower

In 1271, when Marco Polo set sail, Italy consisted of a number of small kingdoms and city-states, some of them under the control of other European countries. Italy would not become a unified country for another 600 years.

Marco's home city of Venice was a successful seaport, which had become an independent republic with its own navy and overseas territory. Over the years, Venice had also grown very wealthy through maritime trade. Venice was perfectly situated to receive Asian goods arriving on the Adriatic Sea and move them into Europe. Each year, a colossal amount of cargo passed through Venice, mostly expensive luxury goods. The harbor taxes alone would have made the city wealthy.

Venice had a great rival, the seaport of Genoa on the opposite side of northern Italy. For several centuries, Venice and Genoa were engaged in a bitter struggle for control of the sea routes in the eastern Mediterranean and for the lion's share of the Asian trade. During the century in which Marco Polo was born, Venice was winning the struggle against the Genoese.

The Mediterranean – a boundary, not a barrier

Then as now, the Mediterranean Sea marked one of the boundaries of Christian Europe known as Christendom. To the north and west lay the Holy Roman Empire and the other Christian kingdoms – England, France, and Spain.

Venetian Ducats

In 1284, while Marco Polo was away, Venice introduced a new coin, the gold ducat. Venetian ducats soon became so popular with international traders that many countries copied them. The copies were not meant as forgeries, it was just that coins that looked like Venetian ducats were the most acceptable form of gold. The ducat was so popular that the design was to remain unchanged for nearly 500 years.

Christian Empires

The ancient Romans created an empire that covered most of Europe and stretched right around the shores of the Mediterranean.

The **Roman Empire** was converted to Christianity by Emperor Constantine I around A.D.330. Little more than a century later, invaders from Central Asia (forerunners of the Mongols) split the empire in two, and conquered the western half (including Rome).

The eastern half became an independent empire ruled from the city of Constantinople. This empire became known as the **Byzantine Empire** (from Byzantium, the Greek name for the city). The Byzantine Empire gave rise to the Greek Orthodox Church, in the same way that the original Roman Empire gave rise to the Catholic Church.

The **Holy Roman Empire** had nothing to do with the ancient Romans. It was "Roman" because it had the blessing of the pope in Rome. The empire was founded by the French king Charlemagne in A.D.800, although France later became an independent country. In Marco Polo's time, the Holy Roman Empire consisted of the whole of central Europe between Denmark and Italy, bordered by France in the west, and by Poland and Hungary in the east. At this time, the Holy Roman Empire was under German control.

To the south and east of the Mediterranean lay the Islamic Empire of the Arabs, including Egypt and Syria.

Across the Mediterranean, Christendom and the Islamic Empire faced each other as bitter enemies. They were divided by religion, language, and culture, but they had one thing in common – the sea. Both sides relied heavily on Mediterranean trade routes. Christian Europe wanted exotic luxuries from Asia such as silks and spices; and Islamic traders needed an outlet for these goods.

The power of Islam

In the fields of astronomy (below), mathematics, and medicine, Islamic scholars were far more advanced than European scholars. In addition, new ideas and technology had arrived from Asia, brought back by Islamic merchants trading with the peoples of that area.

The Islamic Empire was divided into regions that were ruled from cities such as Cairo and Baghdad. Although the empire was divided politically, it was united by very strong ties of religion and culture. All Muslims had to be able to read the Koran (the holy book written in Arabic), so literacy was high. Scholarship was important in the Islamic Empire, and many cities had universities.

The Islamic Empire was also united in its opposition to Christendom. Islamic rulers had long ago given up their dreams of conquering the whole of Europe, and were even prepared to tolerate the existence of a Christian empire. However, they were not prepared to yield any territory to the Christians. Opposition turned to armed conflict when Christian rulers laid claim to the city of Jerusalem on the grounds that it was a holy place

Christian knights embarking for the Crusades.

for Christians. The wars that followed between the Christians and the Islamic Empire are known in Europe as the Crusades.

The Crusades

In 1099, on instructions from the pope in Rome, the First Crusade invaded the Islamic Empire and established a number of independent kingdoms along the Mediterranean coast. For the next two centuries, European armies had to fight a series of Crusades (seven in all) to protect these Christian kingdoms.

In 1204 the Fourth Crusade captured the city of Constantinople and broke up the Byzantine Empire. Venice had helped the Crusaders by supplying ships and food to the Christian armies. As a reward, Venice was granted control of Constantinople and parts of the former Byzantine Empire. Venice now had direct access to the trade routes of Asia.

Constantinople – Istanbul – has been an important city for more than 2,000 years.

European trade

Christendom was linked together by trade as well as by religion. Europe was prosperous, with an expanding population. Some people lived in cities, but most still lived and worked in the countryside. The European economy was based on agricultural produce. Woolen cloth from England, wine and cheese from France, olive oil from Italy, and hams from Germany were some of the bases for trade.

At this time, most of the luxuries in life – from spices to embroidered silk and fabulous jewels – came from Asia. But Asia meant nothing to the people of Europe. As far as they were concerned, these luxury goods came from Venice.

Rich Europeans loved to clothe themselves in exotic silks (below). The silks came from China, along the Silk Road.
(bottom) Buddhist buildings thought to be on the site of a command post on the Silk Road.

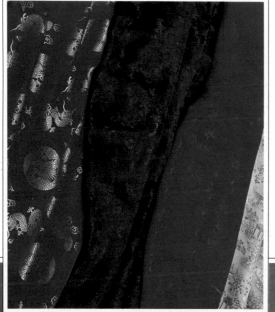

The Silk Road

Not even the Venetian merchants knew where their goods really came from. What is more, they certainly did not realize that they were on the receiving end of a trade network that was already some 1,500 years old.

The overland trade between Europe and Asia began in the period following the death of Alexander the Great in 323 B.C., when Greek kings ruled as far to the east as Afghanistan. Rich Europeans were delighted with the silk fabrics from China, and gladly paid for them in gold and silver coins. The trade expanded under the Romans, but then declined. The rise of the

Religion on the Silk Road

Silks were not the only cargo that traveled along the Silk Road. Religions were also carried overland, but eastward, in the opposite direction to that of silk.

Christianity began to travel down the Silk Road around A.D.500. Most of the Christians who took their faith into China were Nestorians, who belonged to a branch of Christianity that was not recognized by the rest of the Church. Often they moved eastward to escape persecution by other Christians. They built churches along the Silk Road in China, and in other parts of eastern Asia. Two centuries later, Islam was also carried along the Silk Road. Muslim merchants traveled to China and were permitted to set up trading posts in certain cities.

Islamic Empire meant that the trade routes were cut off before they reached Europe.

The Silk Road that brought exotic fabrics from China was just one of several important trade routes from Asia. Other routes carried spices and jewels from India and incense from southern Arabia (the area that includes present-day South Yemen and Oman). All of these routes converged in the Middle East, which was then under the control of the Islamic Empire. Europeans had to trade through Islamic middlemen who kept all the best goods for themselves.

A new power in the East

In 1258 the situation changed completely when, for the first time, the whole of the Silk Road came under the control of a single ruler, Kublai Khan. The newly-established Mongol Empire stretched from the Pacific Ocean to the Middle East. The Mongols were eager to trade directly with Europe, and they were curious about European religion. Their emperor had heard about Christianity, and wanted to learn more. And this is where the Polos reenter the story.

When Marco's father, Niccolo, traveled to China for the first time, he was welcomed by the emperor, who asked Niccolo to deliver a message to the pope. Kublai Khan asked that the pope send Niccolo back to China with 100 Christian priests.

Just before Niccolo set out for China for the second time, a new pope was elected. The pope was unable to organize a party of 100 priests at short notice, but he did send two monks to accompany the Polos with friendly messages for the emperor. The pope knew that there was little chance of converting the Mongols to Christianity, but he did not want to offend Kublai Khan by ignoring the request completely. In any case, according to Marco, the monks ran away soon after the journey began.

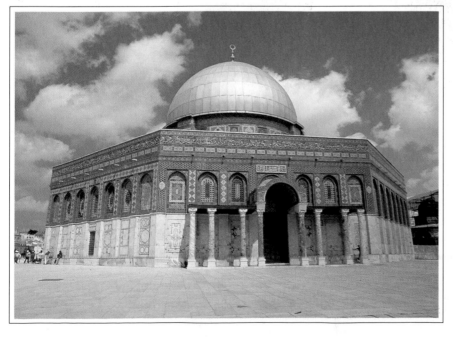

Horizons
You could find out about these people who all lived at around the same time as Marco Polo: Frederick Barbarossa (Holy Roman emperor); Richard the Lionheart (King Richard I of England); Saladin (Islamic sultan of Egypt); the Knights of St. John of Jerusalem and the Knights Templar; troubadours (medieval poets).

A mosque in Jerusalem. Marco visited the city on his way to China.

Modes of Travel

Roman war galley.

Naval power

Venice had grown rich because of its great fleet of merchant ships, but the source of the city's power was the Venetian Navy. The merchants relied on a strong navy to protect them from Genoese ships and Islamic pirates. In turn, the navy relied on the strong muscles of its sailors. The Venetian galley, the warship that dominated the Mediterranean at this time, was powered by a crew of highly trained oarsmen.

The design of the galley had changed little since the Roman Navy ruled the waves, 1,000 years before Marco Polo was born. A typical galley was about 116 feet long, but was quite narrow, being only about 18 feet wide. There was a ram, a kind of pointed iron beam for cutting or piercing enemy ships, above the waterline at the bow, and a small raised platform at the stern for fighting men. In keeping with the Mediterranean tradition, the galley was carvel-built; this means that the planks of the hull were laid edge to edge, not overlapping.

When winds were favorable, one or two masts could be raised, and lateen sails rigged. Roman galleys had used a square sail, but the Venetians had copied the triangular lateen sail from Islamic dhows. While sailing, the galley was steered by two large paddles, one on either side of the stern. When there was no wind, or when going into battle, the galley reverted to oar power. Before gunpowder was introduced, sea battles took place at close quarters, and ramming and boarding were the main tactics used. This style of fighting meant that warships had to be able to change direction quickly, which was not always possible for a sailing ship dependent on the wind.

The galley was a superb warship, but it was too narrow to carry much cargo. Venetian

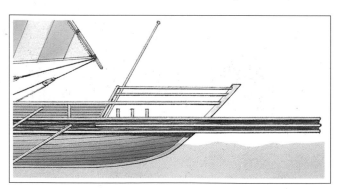

Roman galleys had a ram below the waterline. By the 13th century, rams were placed above the waterline and may also have been used as fighting platforms.

merchant ships were generally much wider than galleys, and they relied on sail power alone. Most had only one mast and a single square sail, and because of their width they were very slow and difficult to handle. Like all sailing ships, they were also liable to stop when the wind dropped.

This defect was overcome by the development of the galeasse, which was making its first appearance around Marco Polo's time. The galeasse was midway between a galley and a sailing ship, and was wide enough to carry a useful amount of cargo. Most of the time, the galeasse sailed with a pair of lateen sails. However, if the wind died a team of rowers would take over.

A Venetian war galley

The war galley, with the ram as its main armament, was one of the most successful warship designs ever built. It was used in Mediterranean navies – with very few changes – from before A.D.300 to after A.D.1700. The introduction of gunpowder marked the start of the galley's decline as a warship. The galley's shape was unsuitable for carrying large numbers of cannons.

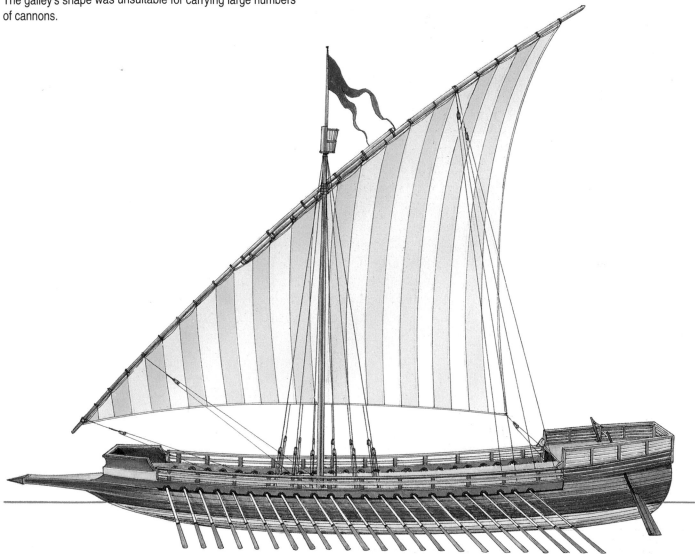

These 16th-century galleys (on the left and right of the picture) had changed little from Marco Polo's time.

The Venetian galley was carvel-built: the planks of the hull were laid edge to edge. The joints became watertight as the planks swelled in the water.

The dhow

The navies of the Islamic Empire also used war galleys, but their most important ship was the dhow, which could be used for both trade and war. The dhow is a small sailing ship with a square stern, a short keel, and a long curved bow. There is usually a single mast rigged with a lateen sail, and it is this that makes the dhow such an efficient sailing craft.

The triangular lateen sail was developed by the Arabs in Roman times. Like a square sail, it hung from a wooden pole called a yard that was attached to the mast, but there the similarity ends. With a square sail, the yard hangs horizontally across the line of the boat, and is only really efficient when the wind is blowing from behind. With a lateen sail, the yard hangs along the ship's line, with one end almost touching the deck. Rigged in this way, the triangular sail can take advantage of winds that blow from the sides.

The lateen sail was particularly useful in the ever-changing winds of the Mediterranean, and this is why the Venetians adopted it for their galleys and galeasses. However, they could not make use of all its advantages. The dhow's short keel enabled it to maneuver very quickly when under sail. The design of the galley required long straight sides for rowers; this meant a long keel which was much less maneuverable.

Dhows are still used in the Indian Ocean. These craft were built in Kenya.

Navigation

The Venetians and their Islamic rivals shared a very old tradition of Mediterranean seafaring. Their ancestors had long ago learned to navigate this large sea, following the coast by day, and steering by the stars at night. Every mile of the coastline had long since been explored and was known in detail. However, such knowledge was of limited use until it could be set down accurately on a chart or map. This was not possible until the magnetic compass became widespread. The compass was originally invented in China, and it slowly traveled westward, first through the Islamic Empire, finally reaching Europe a short time before Marco Polo was born. Interestingly, he makes no mention of a compass, either on Chinese or Venetian ships, but we know of its existence from other evidence. By around 1300, Italian mapmakers were producing charts using information from ships' logbooks. These charts were called portolan charts (from *portolano*, the Italian word for logbook). Portolan charts gave an accurate picture of the Mediterranean coastline, and more importantly they gave compass bearings. A series of lines radiating from various ports enabled navigators to work out a suitable course between any two places.

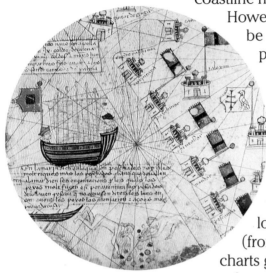

Part of a portolan chart, the Catalan Atlas (see page 41).

The dhow was used throughout the Islamic Empire, in the Persian Gulf, and along the coast of the Indian Ocean, as well as in the Mediterranean. All dhows were roughly similar, but there were one or two variations. Around the port of Hormuz in Persia, Marco Polo noted that the dhows were built without nails. Instead, the planks of the hull were sewn together with tough string made from coconut fibers. These were liable to break, and local sailors carried inflatable leather bags, which they blew up and used as floats if their dhow fell apart at sea.

Trans-Asia caravan

As a Venetian, young Marco had the sea in his blood. A long sea voyage would not have seemed anything out of the ordinary, but nothing in his experience could have prepared him for what was to come. Eventually he was to travel nearly 15,000 miles, several times the distance from Venice to Constantinople, and much of it by land. Mile by slow mile, the outward journey was to take a total of three years.

The Polos were taken along the ancient Silk Road (see page 10), and their means of transportation was equally ancient – animal power pure and simple. Marco says little about his traveling companions or their means of transportation, but it is unlikely that their party traveled alone. They almost certainly joined up with a succession of animal caravans. No single caravan ever made the whole journey between the Mediterranean and China.

A camel caravan in the Gobi Desert.

An old caravansary in Syria.

Goods were carried by a series of caravans operating between cities. A caravan might consist of up to 2,000 animals, some carrying supplies but most loaded down with trade goods. Long-distance travelers were a rarity.

For comfort, the Venetians would have preferred to ride on horseback, but this was not always possible. The animals used in a particular caravan depended on the region and the terrain — dromedaries in the sandy deserts of northern Arabia, donkeys and mules in the mountains of Persia, and Bactrian camels across the high deserts of Afghanistan. In Central Asia, goods and passengers may have been loaded together onto large wooden oxcarts.

A caravan moved in stages of a day's travel, which was a very flexible unit of distance. When darkness fell, it was time to make camp, eat, and sleep, ready for an early start. With good planning, the day's journey would bring the travelers to a caravansary, a resting place for caravans, which was a combination of hotel, restaurant, and information center.

At the caravansary, the travelers could eat and sleep in relative comfort and get news of the road ahead. A large caravansary might have a bathhouse, and keep a stock of replacement animals and harness, and it might provide musical entertainment. The biggest caravansaries were located where the Silk Road branched. Others were located near religious shrines, or at frontier posts where road taxes were collected. In the more remote regions, the caravansary also provided protection. Some had a small garrison of soldiers to deter bandits and keep order.

Chinese roads and rivers

After three years of travel across the wastelands of Central Asia, it was hard not to be impressed with China. The ancient road system had been completely restored by the new rulers. Trees had been planted at regular intervals on both sides of all main highways so that travelers should not lose their way. In dry areas, where trees were a rarity, roads between cities were marked instead by mounds of stones. Local officials were appointed to maintain the roads and make sure that the stones did not tumble down. Good roads were vital to the administration of so vast a country as China at a time when a man on horseback was the fastest and surest method of sending a message. The emperor's postal service alone used some 200,000 horses. Good roads also brought other benefits. Soldiers could reach any trouble spot quickly, merchants could transport goods and materials, farmers could move herds and crops, and taxes could be collected.

Rivers were also important, especially the great Yellow River and the Yangtse River. For centuries, Chinese rivers had been used as highways by a variety of flat-bottomed boats, traveling between inland ports, as well as to and from the sea. The traffic on one of the lesser rivers astounded Marco Polo. He wrote: "so much shipping that no one who has not seen it could believe it, the amount of merchandise transported by this multitude of craft is simply staggering."

A traditional Chinese riverboat.

The Grand Canal is still in use today.

On the larger Yellow River, Marco estimates that there were as many as 15,000 river craft, all of them belonging to the emperor. Many were troop transports of a standard size, each with a crew of 20 sailors and carrying 15 fully-equipped cavalrymen and their horses. The Yangtse River, China's longest river, had the largest ships, some of them carrying 200 tons of cargo, by Marco's estimate. Although these ships had a mast and sail, this was really an auxiliary power source. On the upstream journey, these heavy cargo ships were dragged by teams of horses on the bank using ropes of braided bamboo. Coming downstream, the ships would usually rely on the current.

Inland waterways were so important to China that previous emperors had constructed a series of canals by linking together rivers and lakes with artificial channels. These, too, had recently been restored to their former glory and the Grand Canal now connected the capital, Peking, to the mouth of the Yangtse River. A wide paved road ran along the side of the Grand Canal for use by carts and animals.

Oceangoing ships

In addition to many thousands of river craft, China also had a fleet of larger, seagoing ships. The biggest of these had a crew of up to 300 men, and were used to transport goods to and from India. It was on one of these ships, which are now known as junks, that

Marco made his journey home. Junks had developed from riverboats, but had a keel to make them more stable at sea. As a result, the largest seagoing junks could not enter shallow river estuaries, and had to anchor offshore while goods and passengers were ferried out to them.

A typical seagoing junk was about 100 to 130 feet long, and had a fat, rounded shape with a square bow overhanging the water. The hull was made with a double thickness of planks nailed together. There was a single deck around which were arranged cabins for merchants and travelers.

Trading junks rarely sailed alone, and usually made up small convoys of about a dozen ships of differing sizes. The largest ships would sail with up to ten smaller boats lashed to their sides. These smaller boats were used for fishing during the voyage, and could be used to tow the junk if the wind failed completely.

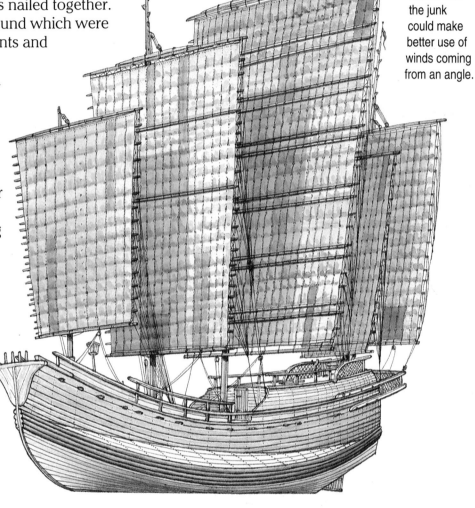

Normally the junk sailed with four masts, but two others could be raised if required. Each mast held a single square sail. The sail was stiffened by a series of horizontal bamboo poles. The bamboo stiffening meant that the junk could make better use of winds coming from an angle.

Below deck, the interior of the ship was divided into a number of watertight compartments, which could be sealed off if the hull was damaged and began to leak.

An important advantage of the junk, over its Islamic and European counterparts, was steering by means of a single rudder hanging from the stern instead of two steering oars. This innovation had only just appeared in the Islamic Empire, and was almost completely unknown in Europe.

The Travels of Marco Polo

Some Middle Eastern cities have changed little since Marco Polo's day.

A Christian beginning

After arriving in Acre on the Palestine coast, the Polos continued their journey in royal style, in a fast galley provided by the Christian king of Armenia. However, this voyage was just a short hop along the coast to the port of Ayas. From there they continued overland and rode eastward through Armenia.

At first the countryside was not very different from home. The plants and trees were typical of the Mediterranean region, and the road took the Polos past monasteries and churches. Somewhere to the north lay Mount Ararat, where Noah's Ark is supposed to have settled after the Flood. Farther on near the Caspian Sea, Marco reports that a wonderful oil seeped from the ground. The local people burned the oil in lamps. Today, this district is known as the Baku oilfield.

Turning south, the travelers began to notice more differences. They were now passing through the heart of the Islamic Empire. Mosques replaced churches, and the climate became hotter and drier. From city to city they traveled, until they came to Kerman in Persia, which lay at the crossroads of several caravan routes. The warehouses of Kerman held spices from India, metalwork from Damascus, and incense from Oman, as well as silks and porcelain from China.

The center of a salt desert is one of the most inhospitable places in the world. Even the water is not fit to drink.

The edge of the known world

Ahead of them lay the great salt desert of central Persia, known as the Kavir, in what is now Iran. This is one of the most inhospitable places in the world. Much of the land is covered with a crust of salt crystals, perhaps from a dried-out sea. In some places the salt crust is thick and safe for people to walk on, but elsewhere it is wafer-thin. Here, the unwary traveler may break through the crust and sink into a sticky bog beneath. Between the salt flats run lines of barren, rocky hills.

Like all deserts, the Kavir has very little water. Even if the traveler finds water, it is usually not fit to drink because of the salt and other minerals. Marco reports how swallowing even the smallest mouthful would make a person violently sick for days. The shortest route across the Kavir took 14 days, and there were only

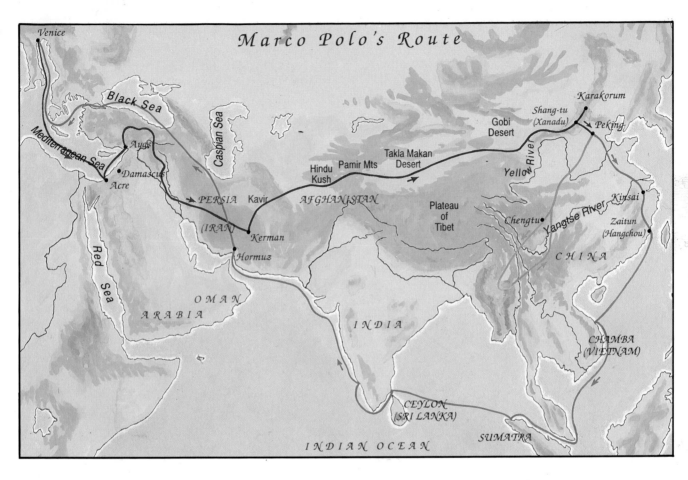

two places where drinking water could be obtained. The Kavir marked the edge of the known world for Christians.

Mountains and deserts

Marco and his companions now climbed up into the unknown wilderness of Afghanistan. They rode on through narrow gorges and snowbound passes, and over stretches of freezing desert, constantly under threat of attack from bandits. By day they were burned by the sun, and at night they shivered and froze. To Marco's astonishment, after many weeks of travel across the uplands of Afghanistan they began to climb even higher, "so high that this is said to be the highest place in all the world," he proudly reports.

He was not far wrong. These were the Hindu Kush mountains, and just to the south stands K2, which at 28,400 feet is the second highest mountain on earth. To the north were the Pamir mountains, which rise to 23,100 feet. Marco Polo was the first European to report the existence of the Pamirs, and they were to remain unexplored for another 600 years.

Marco's route took him through high mountain passes in Afghanistan.

Descending slowly, the Polos crossed the Oxus River and followed the southern branch of the Silk Road, which clung to the foothills of the Tibetan Plateau along the edge of the cold Takla Makan Desert. They passed through a succession of cities, some of which, like Khotan, were then more than 1,000 years old. Eventually they came to the point where the Takla Makan blends into the Gobi Desert. This was the narrowest crossing point, and even that meant 30 days travel across a trackless wasteland. Marco describes the crossing of this final natural barrier in some detail. Men and animals all rested for at least a week before setting out, and each section of the journey was carefully planned with a definite goal. There were just enough waterholes in the desert to make the crossing possible, but reaching them could sometimes mean traveling nonstop for a day and a night. When they finally rode out of the desert, Marco and his companions found themselves at last in China.

These mountains mark the present-day border between Afghanistan and China.

To Xanadu

During his 15 years in China, Marco Polo traveled far and wide. Yet, as he admits, he saw only parts of this vast country, and only three of his journeys are described in any detail. His first journey was to the north, away from China and into the rolling grassland of Mongolia. Here Marco Polo visited the Mongol capital of Karakorum, which was surrounded by a massive earth rampart. The Mongols were not by nature city-dwellers, and Karakorum had been built more as a symbol of Mongol power than as a working city. The city was situated a long way from trade routes and good farmland, and needed over 500 cartloads of produce a day to keep it supplied.

On his way back, Marco visited Shang-tu, better known as Xanadu. Here the new emperor of China had built a magnificent palace with a huge walled garden full of fountains and fine ornamental trees. The garden was stocked with wild animals and birds, which the emperor hunted with falcons and leopards. During the hottest weather, he stayed in a magnificent summerhouse that had a dome-shaped bamboo framework covered with brilliantly colored silks. This was the "stately pleasure dome" that is referred to in the opening line of Samuel Taylor Coleridge's famous poem *Kubla Khan*.

A patchwork of fields in a river valley in southern China.

From cities to jungles

The next journey was made on official business for the emperor, and took Marco through the heart of China to the far southwest and the borders with Burma and Tibet. At first the going was easy. Shortly after leaving Peking, the road crossed a bridge over the Hun-ho River. The bridge, which was more than 825 feet long and 26 feet wide, was made of marble, and was decorated with pillars and carved lions.

Marco was now entering one of the most heavily

Rice fields in central China.

The Great Goose Pagoda was built more than 600 years before Marco Polo's visit.

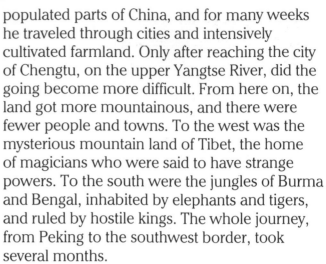

populated parts of China, and for many weeks he traveled through cities and intensively cultivated farmland. Only after reaching the city of Chengtu, on the upper Yangtse River, did the going become more difficult. From here on, the land got more mountainous, and there were fewer people and towns. To the west was the mysterious mountain land of Tibet, the home of magicians who were said to have strange powers. To the south were the jungles of Burma and Bengal, inhabited by elephants and tigers, and ruled by hostile kings. The whole journey, from Peking to the southwest border, took several months.

City of canals

The third journey may well have been part of the Polos' return trip. From Peking, they traveled down the coast of China, all the way to the great port of Zaitun. Journeying southward, they crossed over the Yellow River much sooner than they would today. Since Marco Polo's time, the Yellow River has cut a new course, and now reaches the sea some 300 miles farther south. The Polos passed through many great cities, but none was more impressive than Kinsai, with more than one and a half million houses. Kinsai had been the capital of south China before the Mongols' conquest, and Marco thought it was surely the most marvelous city in the world. It was certainly much larger than any European city. It was situated between a freshwater lake and a river, and had hundreds of canals, which the inhabitants used as often as they used the streets. Across the canals there were some 12,000 bridges, most of them made of stone. The buildings were mainly made of wood, however, and fire was a constant hazard. Fireproof stone towers were built, in which people could store their valuables if fire broke out. From Kinsai, the party traveled down to Zaitun, from where they would set sail.

An arranged marriage

After 20 years away from Venice, the Polos were eager to return home. Their opportunity arose because of an important marriage within the Mongol Empire. A princess from China was traveling to marry the Mongol ruler of Persia, and the bridal party requested the company of the three Venetian travelers.

They started the trip for home in a fleet of 14 oceangoing junks. After two months at sea, they reached the kingdom of Chamba (now South Vietnam). From here they sailed through the Strait of Malacca and along the coast of Sumatra. At this point in the journey, bad weather halted

Divers still collect pearls from the seabed in the traditional manner, without underwater breathing equipment.

The Great Stupa (Buddhist monument) at Sanci in India.

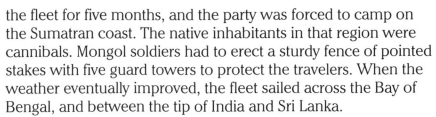

Horizons

These places all lay very close to Marco's long route home: the fortress of Krak des Chevaliers (in Syria); the Great Mosque at Samarra (in Iraq); the city of Samarkand (in Uzbekistan); the Khyber Pass (between Afghanistan and Pakistan); the temple of Angkor Wat (now in Cambodia).

A Chinese vase (right), believed to have been brought back by Marco Polo.

the fleet for five months, and the party was forced to camp on the Sumatran coast. The native inhabitants in that region were cannibals. Mongol soldiers had to erect a sturdy fence of pointed stakes with five guard towers to protect the travelers. When the weather eventually improved, the fleet sailed across the Bay of Bengal, and between the tip of India and Sri Lanka.

Sri Lanka and India

Marco describes Sri Lanka as one of the richest places in the world. The island produced a stream of the finest precious stones: rubies, sapphires, topazes, amethysts, garnets, and pearls. Southern India also produced pearls, and Marco was fascinated by the pearl divers. At the city of Madras, he watched them dive down more than 60 feet, holding their breath while they collected oysters from the seabed. Madras had other attractions for the European visitor. There was a flourishing community of Christians, who claimed that their church was founded by St. Thomas, one of the 12 apostles. The kingdom of Southern India, which Marco called Greater India, was ruled by Hindu kings. (To the north, India was part of the Islamic Empire, and was ruled by the Sultan of Delhi.) Marco understood little of the Hindu religion, but he was impressed by the yogis. These were holy men who meditated and could go without food and water for long periods of time. He also noted that cattle were sacred and were allowed to wander freely.

The final stages

From India, the party sailed westward along a coastline that was a part of the Mongol Empire. Their final landfall was at the port of Hormuz in Persia (now Iran). However, the travels of Marco Polo were still not quite over. From Hormuz, the Venetians had to escort the princess overland to the Caspian Sea, where her future husband was engaged in warfare.

After finally handing over the bride, the Polos made their way overland to the Black Sea. From there they traveled by ship back to Venice. Their arrival in outlandish clothes caused a minor sensation. This turned into a major sensation when they cut open these clothes to reveal that the seams were stuffed with gems. Marco's enthusiastic descriptions of the size and extent of China rapidly earned him the nickname *il Milione* – the man who talks in millions.

What Marco Polo Found

A foreign emperor

Kublai Khan, emperor of China.

The emperor who welcomed the Polos to China was not Chinese. Kublai Khan was a Mongol. The Mongols were a nomadic people who were just one of many tribes inhabiting the great treeless expanse of the Central Asian steppes to the northwest of China. On Marco's journey to the north, he met a party of Mongols still following their traditional way of life. They lived in circular tents, known as gers or yurts, which were made of felt hung over a framework of lightweight poles. The tents were easily dismantled, and were transported on four-wheeled carts drawn by oxen or Bactrian camels. The men, and many of the women and children, rode on horseback. In this manner, they traveled back and forth across the steppes in search of fresh pasture for their animals.

The Mongols were fierce warriors, and for centuries had fought other tribes on the steppes, raiding their camps to steal horses. Mongol soldiers went into battle on horseback and made deadly use of their favorite weapon, a small curved bow. For protection they wore metal helmets and body armor of buffalo hide.

Throughout his book, Marco mistakenly calls Kublai Khan a Tartar. The Tartars were another Central Asian people, who had previously been conquered by the Mongols. No doubt there were many Tartar soldiers in the Mongol Army, and this is probably how the confusion arose.

Traditional circular tents at an encampment in Mongolia.

The rise of Mongol power

About 50 years before Marco Polo was born, the Mongol people had elected a new leader who took the name Ghengis Khan. Khan was the Mongol word for leader. During the next 30 years, Ghengis Khan led his warriors in a series of military campaigns that first conquered north China, and then established a Mongol empire across the whole of Central Asia.

After Ghengis Khan's death, his sons and grandsons continued to expand the empire, with devastating results for the rest of the world. In 1240, a Mongol army invaded eastern Europe and defeated the Polish, German, and Hungarian armies. Europe was

An image of a Mongolian horseman on a 13th-century Persian dish.

saved only by the sudden death of the Khan. In 1258, another Mongol army conquered most of the Islamic Empire, destroying the city of Baghdad which had more than one million inhabitants. In the same year Kublai Khan had begun his successful invasion of southern China, completing the task started by his grandfather Ghengis. Two years later, Kublai was named Great Khan, the supreme ruler of a Mongol empire that stretched from the Pacific Ocean almost to the Mediterranean Sea. The empire was divided into regions, each ruled by a lesser khan, while Kublai devoted his attention to China.

During 60 years of campaigning, the Mongol Army had become a superb fighting machine. Although the Mongols were still horse-soldiers who loved to charge the enemy, they had by now learned the arts of siege warfare and diplomacy. In 1279, southern China was finally defeated, and the whole of China was once again united under a single ruler.

Emperor of China

In addition to being the Mongol supreme leader, Kublai also

A 13th-century European painting of Kublai Khan greeting Marco and his companions.

became the emperor of China, and this called for a different approach. Traditionally, the Mongols treated a conquered people very severely, stealing everything that could be stolen, and burning the rest. However, Kublai Khan realized that this approach would not work in China. The Chinese were settled farmers, and would be worth far more in the long run if they were allowed to carry on farming in peace. So instead of pillaging the country, Kublai simply took over the imperial government and collected taxes just like the emperors before him had done.

Minority rule

At this time, China had a population of about 130 million people, and by comparison the Mongol people were very few in number. In general, the Mongol invasion made very little difference to the ordinary citizens of China – the farmers, the craftworkers, and the civil servants who ran the administration. The victorious warlords may have replaced the Chinese aristocracy, but their conquest had little effect on everyday life. The Mongols were never more than the thinnest layer on the surface of Chinese society.

Kublai Khan had built a new capital city called Khan-balik on the outskirts of Peking. He ruled China from a sumptuous palace in the capital. Next in line to the emperor were 12 Mongol barons, each in charge of a province. Under the barons were lesser officials such as the governors of cities, and many of these were Mongol. But that was as far as it went. The vast majority of government officials were Chinese.

Imperial administration

Making China work efficiently as a single unit required a huge administration employing hundreds of thousands of officials of every rank. From court historians and accountants to lowly officials in charge of street cleaning, the imperial civil service was the second biggest employer in China after farming.

Over the centuries, the Chinese had developed a system to recruit the cleverest people for the emperor's service. Each year, examinations were held in every school in China, and only the most able pupils were selected for further education. After they had mastered the skills of reading and writing, they received more specialized training for their future official positions. The size and scope of Chinese administration was hard to grasp, even in Marco Polo's day. Some idea of the scale of the numbers involved can be obtained from Marco's calculation of the emperor's income from a single city. In one year, Marco calculated, the emperor received the equivalent of 15 million Venetian gold pieces – an immense fortune in European terms.

Writing

Chinese writing is very different from the writing used in the U.S. and Europe or in Islam. It is also much more difficult to learn.

European languages are written from left to right in an alphabet containing about 25 consonants and vowels. Arabic, the language of the Islamic world, is written right to left in an alphabet of 28 consonants, the vowels being represented by dots. The European and Arabic alphabets are related, and evolved from the same ancient alphabet.

Chinese writing evolved separately and is written vertically using up to 60,000 different characters. Some of the characters stand for individual words, some for parts of words, and some just for sounds. Even everyday writing, such as a shopping list or a simple letter, uses about 4,000 individual characters. To make it more difficult, in Marco Polo's time the Chinese used several different scripts. A particular character could be written in at least four different styles: seal, orthodox, cursive, and grass.

Seal script was used for seals and official texts, and was cut in stone and metal with a chisel. Orthodox script was used in government papers and books. It was written with a brush and red or black ink. Cursive script was simpler and quicker to write and was used for notes, letters, and rough drafts. It was written with a brush and ink. Grass script was a decorative version of cursive writing.

The character for "horse" in four different scripts

seal	orthodox	cursive	grass

This design of the cash coin remained unchanged for more than 1,200 years.

In 221 B.C., the first emperor of China introduced the cash coin, a round bronze coin with two characters, one on either side of a square hole. The coin was so popular that it was issued for the next eight centuries. In A.D. 626, the design was altered to include a date, which meant having four characters, one on each side of the hole. This design was to remain unchanged until the last cash coin was minted at the beginning of the 20th century.

The lure of the known

As the first European traveler to visit Asia, Marco Polo was in a sense the first Western tourist. Like tourists today, he was overwhelmed by the scale and magnificence of the cities and palaces that he saw. However, he was also a merchant's son, so it is not surprising that the things that interested him most were the most familiar – the luxury goods of the Asian trade. Throughout his travels, he catalogs in great detail the sources of the finest textiles, gems, and spices. These are some of the items in his lists:

Textiles
Fustian (a heavy cotton and wool fabric) – from Tibet
Buckram (stiffened cotton or linen) – from Madras in India
Yazdi (patterned silk) – from Yazd in Persia
Cloth of gold – from Georgia in Russia
Mosulin (silk and gold fabric) – from Mosul in Iraq
Brocade (fabric woven with a raised design) – from Baghdad in Iraq
Camel hair rugs – from Mongolia
Sable furs – from Siberia
Carpets – from Turkey

Gems
Diamonds – from central India
Rubies – from Sri Lanka
Emeralds – from southern India
Sapphires – from Afghanistan
Lapis lazuli – from Mongolia
Jasper – from Central Asia
Pearls – from southern India and Sri Lanka

Spices
Cloves – from Sumatra
Cinnamon – from Tibet
Nutmegs – from Java
Ginger – from southern China
Pepper – from India

Money was another familiar area of interest. Marco Polo does not mention coins, but he greatly admired the Chinese paper money. These printed paper notes, stamped with a value in bronze, silver, or gold, had been introduced a short while before the Mongol invasion, and Kublai Khan encouraged their use. However, in the more remote parts of China, Marco noted that people still used primitive money such as blocks of salt or cowrie shells.

Like tourists today, Marco liked to know how much things cost compared with home – in several places he records how many partridges he could buy for the equivalent of a Venetian silver *grosso*.

True or false?

Not everything in Marco Polo's book is true. He repeats as fact many of the traveler's tall tales and myths that he heard during his journeys. However, he does reveal the truth behind one particular myth, that of the salamander.

The salamander is an amphibian, which was widely believed to be fire-resistant, and even to live inside fires. The belief arose because salamanders often hide beneath the bark of logs, and then rush out when the logs are placed on a fire. In fact, salamanders are no more fireproof than any other animal, but something else is – asbestos. As Marco gleefully reveals, "salamander is not a beast as commonly believed," but a type of rock. Crushing this rock produced asbestos fibers which could be woven into a white cloth that was completely resistant to fire. Marco reports that one of these cloths had been sent as a gift to the pope in Rome.

Discoveries and souvenirs

Surprisingly, Marco Polo writes about very few things that were completely new to him, but he does describe the following:
Coal When Marco first saw "stones that burn like logs" in northern China, he was amazed – he had never seen a coal fire before. This was a result of living in Venice, which has a warm Mediterranean climate. Had Marco lived in London at this time, he would have found coal almost as commonplace as in China.
Tattooing Although this is an ancient form of adornment, it seems to have been a novelty to Marco Polo, and he describes the process in some detail. The tattoos were in black ink only, usually on the arms and legs. He states that people traveled great distances in order to visit the best tattooists.
Sago Marco calls sago "flour from trees." It is the dried, powdered pith of the sago palm, a tree that Marco found in Sumatra. He thought it was a real marvel, and took a sample – perhaps some powder, or even a tree seedling – back to Venice with him.

Although the Polos may have brought back all kinds of riches, very little is actually recorded. Apart from the sago, this is what we know Marco brought back with him:
Seeds of the brazilwood tree, used for making red dye. The seeds were planted on Marco's return, but they wouldn't grow.

The European salamander. Folk legend held that salamanders could withstand flames. Marco correctly reported that the legendary salamander was in fact asbestos.

Domesticated yaks in Mongolia.

Yak wool Marco saw yaks in Mongolia. The wool on their necks is very long and fine and people in Italy were amazed at the quality of this wool.

Soil from the grave of St. Thomas in Madras. Marco belonged to the Christian world of Europe, and the supposed presence of one of Christ's apostles in distant India obviously made a great impression on him.

What was left out

The Japanese copied the Chinese tea-drinking habit and tea may still be served with elaborate ceremony.

To the people of 14th-century Europe, Marco Polo's book was a catalog of strange and wonderful things. What strikes a modern reader as being strange are the things that Marco Polo did not mention. For some reason, he left out some of the most interesting aspects of Chinese civilization.

From his account, it would appear that Marco never had a cup of tea during all his years in China. He describes how the Mongols made a drink called koumiss from horse's milk, but he makes no mention at all of tea, which was completely unknown to Europeans of the time.

Tea is first mentioned in Chinese books around A.D.350, but tea drinking probably began much earlier in the far south of the country near the border with Burma. The use of tea had been spread through China by Buddhist monks, and tea became so popular

In Khotan in China, paper is still made as it was when Marco Polo visited.

▲ Stripping mulberry bark.

▲ Pounding the bark to separate the fibers.

that the government put a tax on it. By the time of Marco's visit, tea drinking was a common custom in China, and the best teas were often served with elaborate ceremony.

Why did he fail to write about tea? Perhaps he didn't like the taste. As a result of his omission, Europe remained ignorant of tea for another 250 years. Tea is not mentioned in European books until 1559.

The printed page

Printing is another item missing from Marco's list of wonders. He refers to printed paper money, made from mulberry bark, but says nothing about the printing process or about printed books. The technique of printing on paper was developed in China sometime before A.D.500. By A.D.900, whole books were being printed from wooden blocks one page at a time. All the words on a page were carved into the same block of wood. During the next 200 years, Chinese printers experimented with movable type, where each word or character was molded into a separate block of wood, metal, or pottery. The individual blocks could then be arranged to make up a page of text. All of this had taken place before Marco Polo's visit, yet Chinese printing either failed to impress him, or escaped his notice entirely. Perhaps he did not look at the books because he knew that he would not be able to read them.

In Europe, a few artists were working out how to print pictures, but books still had to be copied out by hand. The earliest known printed book in Europe was not produced until around 1455, when Johannes Gutenberg printed the Bible in Germany.

▲ Boiling the bark into a pulp.

► Lifting the paper-making frame from the prepared pulp.

► Peeling off the finished paper.

Secret weapon

The most interesting of Marco's omissions is gunpowder. The secret of making gunpowder was well-known to the Chinese, who used it for fireworks. However, gunpowder also had a more sinister side – it could be used for making weapons. The Mongol Army had used gunpowder rockets in warfare during the 1240s, and had passed on the secret to the Islamic Empire.

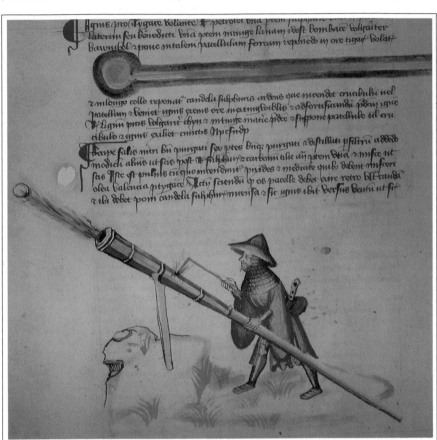

One of the very first European cannons, painted on a 14th-century manuscript.

The arrival of gunpowder in Europe is still clouded in mystery. Cannons were first used in European warfare around 1340, and it is likely that the secret of gunpowder was obtained from the Islamic Empire. The information certainly did not come from Marco Polo's book, yet surely he must have seen gunpowder being used. He claims to have accompanied a Mongol army into battle, but there is no mention of the new wonder weapon.

This is perhaps not that surprising. Remember that he wrote his book as a prisoner of war in a Genoese cell. Marco was a loyal Venetian, so he was not likely to tell the enemy about a powerful new weapon.

Distant geography

When Marco Polo's book was first published it was called *A Description of the World*, and this is exactly what it set out to be. Marco described not only the countries he visited, but also the even more distant lands that he only heard about. He describes Siberia, to the north of Mongolia, with its lakes and marshes, and savage tribes that rode on reindeer instead of horses. He explains that after 80 days' journey to the north a traveler would reach a cold, harsh coastline edging what we now call the Arctic Ocean. He also describes Korea and Japan (where "the buildings were roofed with gold") to the east, places that were still unknown in Europe. He tells of the exotic islands of Madagascar and Zanzibar, off the coast of Africa, and of the Christian kingdom of Ethiopia.

At the time, many people did not believe much of what they read in his book – it all seemed too fantastic. Today, we know that much of what he described really was true.

Oriental Civilization

A bronze wine cooler made during the Shang dynasty about 3,000 years ago.

In 206 B.C., Shihuangdi died. In 1975, his tomb was discovered by archaeologists. Buried with Shihuangdi were 8,000 life-size clay statues, each representing a warrior in his army. Chinese records show that it took more than 700,000 workers to construct his tomb.

Dynasty and wealth

By the time of Marco Polo's visit, the Chinese could already trace their civilization back over 3,000 years. They divide their history into periods that are named after the ruling dynasty (a dynasty is a series of leaders belonging to the same family).

The first of these was the Shang dynasty, which ruled in the northeast between 1800 and 1028 B.C. Many of the essentials of Chinese culture were present in Shang times. Farmers grew rice and millet, and silkworms were raised on farms to make silk. Metalworkers made elaborate ceremonial vases in bronze. But the most important achievement of the Shang dynasty was the development of Chinese writing (see box on page 28).

The Shang dynasty was followed by the Chou dynasty. The Chou emperors gradually extended their borders southward and westward, doubling their empire's size. Around the end of the dynasty, iron making was introduced and quickly became widespread. Chinese smiths were highly skilled, and they were making cast-iron tools and weapons almost 2,000 years before cast iron was first made in Europe. Once iron tools were available, more land could be cleared for agriculture, and more food could be grown.

The first emperor of China

Around 770 B.C., the Chou empire began to break up into more than 100 small kingdoms, which were constantly at war with each other. For this reason, the Chinese refer to the next 550 years as the Warring States period. Gradually, as the stronger states conquered the weaker ones, the number of warring states became fewer, until one of them emerged as the most powerful. This was the state of Chin, from which China takes its name. By 221 B.C., Shihuangdi, the king of Chin, had become the emperor of China. This date is generally taken to mark the formal beginning of the Chinese Empire, as opposed to the Shang and Chou empires that came before.

The Great Wall

Without doubt, the biggest omission from Marco Polo's book was China's Great Wall, much of which is still standing. The Great Wall is about 30 feet high, and wide enough for six horsemen to ride abreast. It stretches for more than 1,200 miles and is by far the biggest structure ever built by human beings.

Most of the wall was built by slave labor at the command of the emperor Shihuangdi around 215 B.C., although some parts are even older. The Great Wall runs along what was China's northern border, and it was intended to keep out invaders from Central Asia. Sections of the wall had been demolished when Ghengis Khan invaded China, more than 50 years before Marco's visit. This is probably why he did not notice it when he went north.

Han and Tang

The next dynasty was the Han (206 B.C.-A.D.220), which expanded the empire westward to the Takla Makan Desert and southward to the borders of Vietnam. The Han dynasty increased the emperor's powers and there was an increase in long-distance trade with the empires of Persia, Greece, and Rome. Inside China, the most important development of the Han dynasty was probably the invention of paper around A.D.100 (see page 32).

The last emperor of the Han dynasty was overthrown in 220, and China once again became divided into smaller states. The country was not united again until the Tang dynasty took over in 618. During the Tang period, trade and industry once again flourished in China, and the empire became rich and powerful. The Grand Canal was built to transport food from the fertile south to the cities in the north. Increased trade meant that China was open to new influences and new religions. Buddhism filtered in from India, and Islam arrived by sea from Arabia.

Sung splendor

In 907, the Tang dynasty was replaced by the Sung dynasty, which ruled until it was overthrown by the Mongols who founded their own Yuan dynasty. Under the Sung dynasty, the south of China became more important than the north, largely because of its better farmland. This shift to the south meant that the overland trade routes, such as the Silk Road, became less important. Instead, the Sung dynasty preferred to transport goods by water. River traffic increased and many canals were built. The empire also developed a fleet of oceangoing ships which regularly sailed as far as India. The invention of printing allowed books to be mass-produced. This in turn meant that more people were better educated. At the time of the Mongol invasion in 1215, Sung China was a highly civilized empire with a population of well over 100 million.

Silken Wealth

China's wealth came mainly from the trade in silk, a fiber produced by the silkworm. For the first part of its life, the silkworm feeds on the leaves of the mulberry tree. After a few months, it spins itself a cocoon of silken thread from special glands in its body. Inside the cocoon, the caterpillar changes into a moth. If the cocoon is unwound before the moth emerges, the silk thread can be woven into a strong, lightweight fabric.

The Chinese discovered how to make silk nearly 5,000 years ago, but the secret of silk-making was kept hidden from Europe for many years.

In A.D.550, four silkworms were smuggled out of China and taken to the Byzantine emperor, who immediately set up silk farms in what is now Turkey. By Marco Polo's day, silk was being made in parts of Europe, and throughout the Middle East. Most silk, however, still came from China.

Cultivated silkworms are fed on mulberry leaves on Chinese silk farms.

Religions in Asia

Marco Polo knew about only three religions, his own Christianity, Islam, and Judaism. These are the religions of the Mediterranean, and not surprisingly they are closely related and share similar ideas and beliefs. On his travels, Marco met people who followed other religions.

Confucianism The Han dynasty had made Confucianism the official religion of China in 136 B.C. Confucianism is not really a religion, but a code of behavior based on the teachings of Confucius, a thinker, who lived during the Warring States period (see page 34). Confucius taught that the greatest virtues were those of wisdom, courage, humanity and, most of all, obedience. Confucius believed that obedience began in the family, and extended to include obedience to the emperor.

Taoism Confucianism had a Chinese rival in Taoism, which was based on the writings of Lao Tse, who lived around 550 B.C. Followers of Taoism seek the eternal "tao" (which means "way"), a sort of harmony between people and nature. Compared with Confucianism, which is very practical and down-to-earth, Taoism is quite vague and mystical.

Hinduism Hinduism began about 5,000 years ago, developing out of even older beliefs. Hindus believe that the world is ruled by a pantheon, which is a group of gods and goddesses.

Hindus believe that people are born into one of a large number of castes (social classes), and there are strict rules about how people of different castes should behave toward each other. Most Hindus also believe in reincarnation – that is they believe that when a person dies, the soul is born again in another body. By living a good life, and worshiping the gods devoutly, a person might be reborn into a better caste in their next life.

Buddhism Buddhism was founded by Siddhartha Gautama, a prince from Nepal born in 563 B.C., who became a religious teacher. After years of meditation, the prince achieved enlightenment and became known as the Buddha, which means "Enlightened One." The Buddha accepted the Hindu ideas of reincarnation and a great cycle of life, but he rejected the caste system and all of the Hindu gods. Buddhism teaches people not to hate or be greedy. It teaches that by leading a good and holy life, people may progress through many reincarnations until they finally achieve nirvana, a state of absolute peace.

Perhaps Marco Polo was prevented from learning more about these religions because he did not speak Chinese or any Indian language, or perhaps he was just bewildered by the great variety of religious images that he saw. He may also have been confused by the local attitude toward religion. Many Chinese saw nothing wrong with believing in more than one religion, and might be Confucians, Taoists, and Buddhists all at the same time. This situation was completely contrary to Marco Polo's previous experience. He was more used to the bitter rivalries between the Mediterranean religions.

▲ A portrait of Confucius carved into stone.

▲ The Hindu god Vishnu.

▲ A statue of Buddha carved into a Chinese mountainside.

What Happened Later

After Marco left

Kublai Khan died in 1295, the same year that Marco Polo arrived back in Venice. After his death, the Mongols were to rule China for another 70 years, but none of the emperors that followed were as clever as Kublai Khan. During the 1340s, Mongol power was weakened by a series of floods and famines, which led to revolts in southern China. In 1368, the Mongols were overthrown, and replaced by the Chinese Ming dynasty, which was to rule until 1644.

A lion statue (above) and The Temple of Heaven (right) in the Forbidden City, in Peking, which was built by the Ming emperors.

The first Ming emperors had a fairly adventurous overseas policy. They sent men on voyages of long-distance exploration almost a century before the first European explorers set sail. Between 1400 and 1420, Chinese sailors made at least seven voyages, ranging as far as Madagascar and the African coast. These voyages represent the high point of Chinese seafaring. One of the junks involved, the *Cheng Ho*, was said to be over 525 feet in length. This was much larger than any ship built in Europe at that time, and the *Cheng Ho* may well have been the longest sailing ship ever built.

The end of the line

The emperors soon lost interest in the sea because there was too great a danger of foreign influences seeping into China. The Ming dynasty decided that China should go back to looking inward rather than outward. Undisturbed by new ideas from outside, China prospered under the Ming dynasty. Much of the finest Chinese art dates from this period.

In 1644, the Ming dynasty was overthrown by another group of invaders, this time from Manchuria in the far northeast of China. The Manchus, who were to rule China until the beginning of the 20th century, also wanted to keep China looking inward. This policy of keeping China closed to foreigners was to bring the Manchu emperors into conflict with European nations that were anxious for increased trade. During the 17th, 18th, and 19th centuries, Europeans gradually gained a foothold in China and foreign ideas flooded into the country. The Chinese people lost confidence in the rule of the emperors, and at the beginning of the 20th century the last emperor was overthrown. After more than 3,500 years, the long sequence of Chinese dynasties was ended.

A European lady painted on silk by a 19th-century Chinese artist.

A Persian painting of Timur and his court.

The tomb of Timur in Samarkand, in Uzbekistan.

Christianity

There were already Christians in China when Marco Polo visited, but these were Nestorian heretics (see page 11). Kublai Khan was much more interested in the pope in Rome. A religious leader who could send armies against the Islamic Empire was of obvious interest to the Mongol emperor. Kublai did not live to meet the emissaries from the pope who eventually arrived in China, no doubt as a result of the Polos' visit. In 1307, the pope appointed the first Catholic archbishop of Peking, and Christian visitors to China were fairly common until the 1340s, when contact between Europe and China suddenly declined.

Last flourish

As the Mongol Empire disintegrated after Kublai Khan's death, much of the Middle East was absorbed back into the Islamic Empire, and travel through Central Asia became unsafe. By 1350, the Silk Road was virtually closed, and trade was slow to improve. Europe would never again be so closely linked with China as it was at the height of Mongol power. In 1360, another powerful warlord emerged named Timur the Lame, or Tamerlane. He was a ruthless warrior who briefly carved out an empire that included Afghanistan, Pakistan, Persia, and much of southern Russia. However, Mongol power ended with his death in 1405.

One of the consequences of the Mongol Empire was the arrival of the Ottoman Turks in Europe. The Ottomans had originally inhabited a part of the Central Asian steppes, but had been pushed westward by Mongol expansion. They settled in what is now called Turkey, and established the Ottoman Empire at the end of the 13th century. Their empire expanded through conquest, and by 1400 the Ottomans ruled most of Turkey and Greece. In 1402, they conquered Constantinople and renamed it Istanbul. During the next two centuries, the Ottomans extended their empire to include much of the old Islamic Empire, and parts of southern Europe.

Around the Mediterranean

Within three years of arriving home, Marco Polo had been captured in battle by the Genoese, and was dictating his story to a fellow prisoner. After his release, Marco seems to have lived a quiet life, and there is no record of him until his death in 1324. Although the Genoese won an occasional battle against Venice, they lost the long-term struggle. Venice grew stronger, earning enormous wealth from the trade in Asian goods. The Venetian Navy was able to keep Genoese ships out of the eastern Mediterranean. As a result, the Genoese turned their attention to the west, and built up trade with France and Spain.

In the east, Venice was to be engaged in warfare against the Ottoman Turks for the next 150 years. One by one, the Venetian island fortresses fell to the advancing Turks. Venice was not alone in the struggle – the whole of Europe was threatened, on land and at sea. In 1529 the Turks advanced to the gates of Vienna, but were driven back by Christian forces. In 1571, the combined fleets of Spain and Venice defeated the Turks at the naval battle of Lepanto. The advance of the Ottoman Empire was halted, but it was to remain largely intact until the 20th century.

Window on the world

In some ways, it can be said that Marco Polo's journey had little influence on world history. For a short time, trade between China and Italy flourished, and there was briefly an archbishop of Peking, but that is all. Disease (see page 42) and the collapse of the Mongol Empire changed everything.

Marco's journey took place through a unique window of opportunity that existed because of the Mongol Empire. When that empire passed into history, the window was closed. China once again turned its back on the world, and European traders and travelers would never again be welcomed with such open arms.

Although Europe and Asia were once again separated, the knowledge of China and India was not lost. Marco's description of Asia was the only one available, and through his book he more than doubled the size of the known world. This new knowledge was gradually used in maps.

A wealth of imagination

The most important consequence of Marco's journey was that the wealth of India and China now burned bright in the European imagination. Those who dared to dream of spices and silks now knew where these treasures came from. They could point to a place on a map and say, "I want to go there!" However, the overland route was now closed by the empires of Ottoman and Islam. If Europeans wanted to trade directly with Asia, then they would have to trade by sea.

▶ Part of the Catalan Atlas, published in 1375, which was based on the information in Marco's book. Marco (for some reason upside down) is shown traveling the Silk Road.

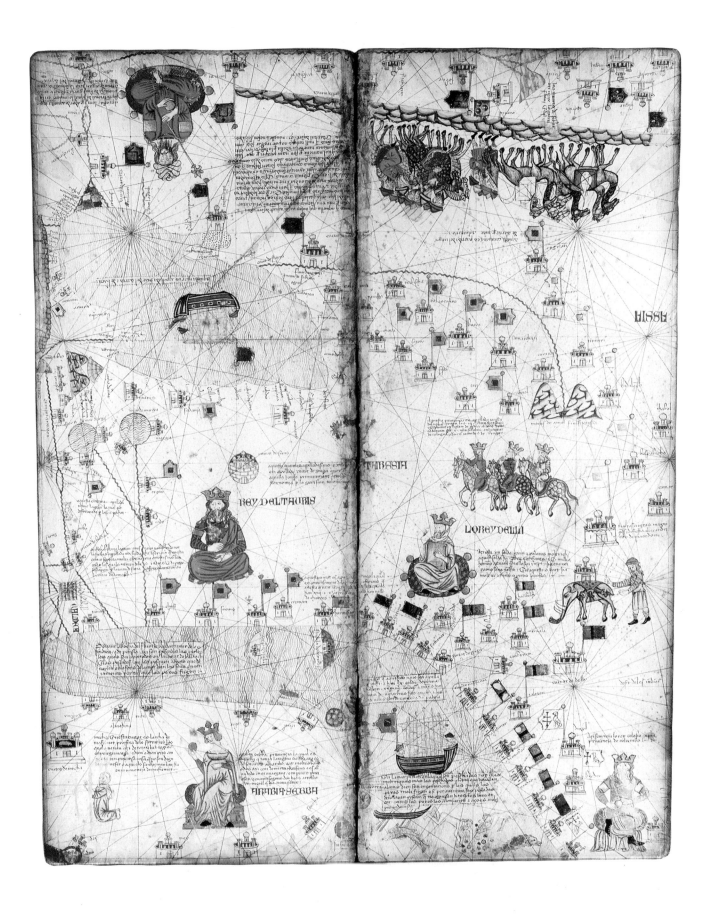

The Black Death

The Silk Road was closed around 1350, when the Mongol Empire collapsed. However, before it closed it carried one last import from Asia to Europe – the Black Death, a form of bubonic plague. The disease causes dark blotches to appear on the victim's body, which is why it was called the Black Death.

Between 1347 and 1350, a massive outbreak of bubonic plague, which had started in China, killed nearly half the people in Europe.

The economic damage to Europe was enormous. Suddenly, there were not enough people to farm all the land and trade also declined. Recovery was slow, and it was not until a century later that Europe began to regain its former prosperity.

The Black Death had nothing to do with Marco Polo; he had been dead for more than 20 years when the disease first appeared in Europe. However, they both traveled the same road. The entry of the Black Death into Europe – from the Black Sea to Constantinople, and then to Italy – followed the same route, but with much greater consequences.

Doctors could do little to help the victims of the Black Death.

Christopher Columbus, who searched for another route to China.

It is little known that when Christopher Columbus arrived in America, he made his crew swear that they were in Asia, because that is where he thought he was. Columbus had reasoned that if the world was a sphere, then he could sail to India and China (in the east) by sailing westward around the world. In his dreams of Asia, Columbus had fallen under Marco Polo's spell, and we know that Columbus carried a copy of *The Travels* with him when he sailed.

Changing times

The story of Columbus belongs to the next chapter of European exploration, when the focus had shifted away from the Mediterranean Sea, and out to the great oceans – first to the Atlantic, and then beyond into the Indian and Pacific. Marco Polo belonged to the Europe of the Middle Ages, which was confined to the Mediterranean. Columbus belonged to a Europe that had recovered from the Black

Death and was entering the modern period, bursting out of the landlocked sea, and out into the world.

The Battle of Lepanto, which saved Europe from the Ottomans in 1571, gave Venice a final moment of glory, but the city's power had already declined. The Mediterranean was no longer the center of the world, and Venetian galleys were not suitable for ocean waves. Spain fought alongside Venice at Lepanto. The difference between the two allies was that Spanish ships also sailed the world's oceans, while Venetian ships were restricted to the Mediterranean. The riches of Asia continued to pour into Europe, but now they were carried by sea. Spain and Portugal replaced Venice and Genoa as the great rivals of maritime trade.

Ibn Battutah - An Islamic Journey

In 1325, a 21-year-old scholar named Ibn Battutah set out from his hometown of Tangiers in Morocco. For the next 29 years he journeyed all over the Islamic Empire from Spain to India, and beyond to China. Like Marco Polo before him, Ibn Battutah produced a book about his travels, and he is famous in the Islamic world. Ibn Battutah kept traveling for his whole life, and covered more than 70,000 miles.

There is no evidence that Ibn Battutah had ever heard of Marco Polo, and he traveled completely independently, yet these two long-distance travelers had much in common.

Horizons

Here are some more cross-connections between Marco's story and later events:

In China Matteo Ricci; the Opium Wars; Hong Kong; the Boxer Rebellion; the Great March.

In India Vasco da Gama; Goa; the East India Company; tea clippers.

Other explorers Bartolomeu Dias; Ferdinand Magellan.

The Battle of Lepanto, 1571, marked the high point of Venetian naval power. This painting shows the victorious fleet returning to Venice in triumph.

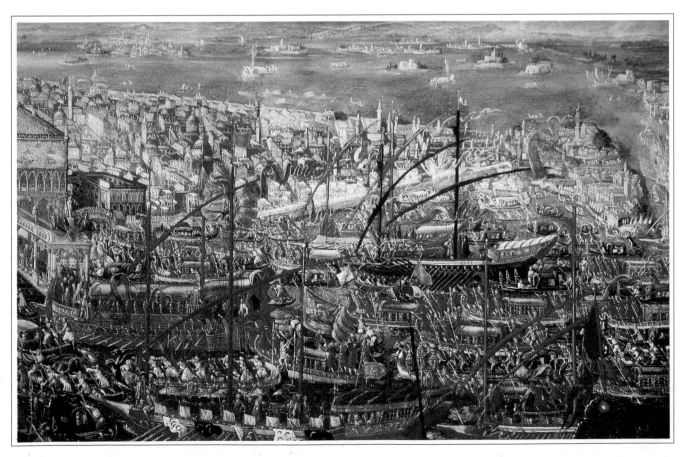

Glossary

Arabia   A large peninsula between Africa and Asia. It is the homeland of the Arab peoples. Today, Arabia is divided into the following countries: Kuwait, Oman, Qatar, Saudi Arabia, the United Arab Emirates, and Yemen.

bow (of ships)   The sloping or curving front portion of a ship's hull.

city-state   An independent state consisting of a single city and its surrounding district.

dynasty   The "family" to which a series of rulers belong.

emissary   Someone sent on a special mission; an official messenger or traveling representative.

empire   A large and powerful state, which may consist of more than one country, that is under the control of a single ruler known as an emperor or empress.

hull   The watertight structure that forms the body, or outer shell, of a ship.

imperial   Belonging to or connected with an empire or an emperor.

keel   A projection from the underside of a ship's hull that keeps the ship stable in the water.

kingdom   A country ruled over by a king or queen.

Mohammed   The prophet who founded the Islamic religion, who died in A.D.632.

mosque   A building that is an Islamic place of worship.

oriental   Belonging to, or coming from, the East (Asia).

republic   A state ruled by an elected president or council.

siege warfare   A type of warfare in which towns and cities are surrounded and are then attacked or starved into submission.

steppes   The natural open grasslands of Central Asia.

stern (of ships)   The rear portion of a ship's hull, often square-cut rather than rounded.

yogi   An Indian holy man who devotes his life to meditation.

Further Reading

Biel, Timothy L. *The Black Death*. Lucent Books, 1989

Brightfield, Richard. *China: Why Was an Army Made of Clay?* McGraw-Hill, 1989

Brown, Stephen F. *Taoism*. Facts on File, 1992

Clooney, Francis X. *Confucianism*. Facts on File, 1992

Cootes, R.J. *Middle Ages*. Longman Pub. Grp., 1989

Corbishley, Mike. *Medieval World*. P. Bedrick Bks., 1993

——— *Middle Ages*. Facts on File, 1990

Dramer, Kim. *Kublai Khan*. Chelsea House, 1990

Greene, Carol. *Marco Polo: Voyager to the Orient*. Childrens Press, 1987

Hoobler, Dorothy and Hoobler, Thomas. *Chinese Portraits*, "Images Across the Ages" series. Raintree Steck-Vaughn, 1993

Humble, Richard. *Travels of Marco Polo*. Watts, 1990

Jackson, Julia A. *Gemstones: Treasures from the Earth's Crust*. Enslow Pubs., 1989

Johnson, Sylvia A. *Silkworms*. Lerner Pubns., 1982

The Late Middle Ages, "History of the World" series. Raintree Steck-Vaughn, 1992

Martell, Mary H. *The Ancient Chinese*. Macmillan, 1992

Noonan, Jon. *Marco Polo*. Macmillan, 1993

Rosen, Mike. *The Travels of Marco Polo*. Watts, 1989

Stefoff, Rebecca. *Marco Polo and the Medieval Explorers*. Chelsea House, 1992

Ventura, Piero. *Venice: Birth of a City*. Putnam, 1988

Index

Kublai Khan, emperor (China), 11, 26, 27, 38, 39

Lao Tse, 37
lateen sails, 12, *13,* 14
Lepanto, Battle of, 40, 43
literacy, Islamic, 8

Madagascar, 33, 38
Madras, 25, 29
Malacca, Strait of, 24
Manchus, rule China, 38
maritime trade, 7, 43
    See also trade
masts, 12, 14, *19*
Mediterranean Sea, *7-8, 21*
merchant ships, Venetian, 12
metal working, 34
millet, 34
Ming emperors, 38
money, Chinese paper, 30, 32
Mongol Empire, 5, 11, 40
Mongolia, 23, 29, *31*
Mongols, 26-27, 38
monks, 11
    Buddhist, 31
mosque(s), *11*, 20, 25
Mosul (Iraq), 29
Mount Ararat, 20
mules, 16

navigation, aids to, 15
Nestorians, 11, 39
Noah's Ark, 20

oarsmen, for galley, 12, 14
oil, 20
olive oil, 10
Oman, 11, 20, *21*
Ottoman Empire, 39
Ottoman Turks, 39, 40
oxcarts, 16
oxen, 26
Oxus River, 22

Pacific Ocean, 11
paddles, 12
Pakistan, 39
palace(s), 23, 27-28
Pamir mountains, 21
pantheon, 37
paper, 32, 35
Peking (China), 18, *21,* 27, *38*
Persia, *21,* 25, 35, 39
    See also Iran
pirates, Islamic, 12
Poland and Polish, 8, 26
Polo, Marco, *4*
    discoveries of, 30-31
    early life of, 6
    as *il Milione,* 25

as prisoner of war, 33
    souvenirs of, *25,* 30-31
    what he found, 26-33
Polo, Niccolo, 6
    and Kublai Khan, 11
porcelain, 20
Portolan charts, 15
Portugal, 43
postal service, Chinese, 17
printing 6, 32, 36

ram, as ship's weapon, 12, 13
Red Sea, *21*
reincarnation, 37
reindeer, 33
religion(s)
    in Asia, 37
    new Chinese, 35
    on Silk Road, 11
rice, *24,* 34
rivers, Chinese, 17-18, *24*
roads, 17
Roman Empire, 8, 35
rudder, *19*
Russia, southern, 39

sable furs, 29
sago, 30
sails, 14, *19*
    See also lateen sails
salamander, 30
salt, as primitive money, 30
salt desert, 20-21
Samarkand, *39*
script, kinds of Chinese, 28
Shang dynasty, 34
Shang-tu, *21,* 23
    See also Xanadu
Shihuangdi, *34*
ships, oceangoing, 18-19, 36
Siberia, 29, 33
Siddhartha Gautama, 37
silk(s), 8, *10, 36*
Silk Road, 10-11, 15, 22, 39, *41*
silkworms, 34, 36
South Yemen, 11
Spain, 7, 40, 43
spices, 8, 10, 11, 20, 29
Sri Lanka, 29
    See also Ceylon
steppes, 26
stone mounds, as markers, 17
Sumatra, *21,* 24, 29
Sung dynasty, 36
Syria, *16*

Takla Makan Desert, *21,* 22, 35
Tamerlane. *See* Timur the Lame
Tang dynasty, 35
Tangiers (Morocco), 43
Taoism, 37

Tartars, 26
tattooing, 30
tea, 31-32
Temple of Heaven, *38*
tents, Mongolian, 26
terrain, and caravans, 16
textiles, 29.
    See also fabrics
Thomas, St., 25, 31
Tibet, 23-24, 29
    plateau, *21,* 22
tigers, 24
Timur the Lame, 39
trade
    Asian, 7
    European, 10
    Han dynasty, 35
    Marco's preoccupation with, 5
    overland European/Asian, 10-11
Trans-Asia caravan, 15-16
transportation, under Sung dynasty, 36
travel, modes of, 12-19
Travels of Marco Polo - A Description of the World, The (Polo), 4, 5
    consequences of, 40
    influence of, 42
troop transports, 18
Turkey, 29, 36, 39

Uzbekistan, 25, *39*

Venice, *21,* 25
    as commercial superpower, 7
    controls Constantinople, 9
    decline of, 43
    Marco's departure from, 6
    navy of, 12
    rivalry of with Genoa, 7, 12, 40
    war galley of, *13*
    wars of against Ottoman Turks, 40
Vietnam, 35
Vishnu, *37*

Warring States period, 34
wine, 10
woolen cloth, 10

Xanadu, 23

yak wool, 31
Yangtze River, 17, 18, *21,* 24
Yazd (Persia), 29
Yellow River, 17, 18, *21,* 24
yogis, 25
Yuan dynasty, 36
yurts (gers), 26

Zaitun (Hangchou), *21,* 24
Zanzibar, 33